A SLIPPERY SLOPE

A SLIPPERY SLOPE

TOON TELLEGEN

Translated by Judith Wilkinson

All rights reserved. No part of this work covered by the copyright herein may be reproduced or used in any means – graphic, electronic, or mechanical, including copying, recording, taping, or information storage and retrieval systems – without written permission of the publisher.

Printed by imprintdigital
Upton Pyne, Exeter
www.digital.imprint.co.uk

Typesetting and cover design by The Book Typesetters
hello@thebooktypesetters.com
07422 598 168
www.thebooktypesetters.com

Published by Shoestring Press
19 Devonshire Avenue, Beeston, Nottingham, NG9 1BS
(0115) 925 1827
www.shoestringpress.co.uk

First published 2023
© Copyright: Toon Tellegen and Judith Wilkinson
© Cover painting: Snow in Central Park, by Robert Henri. 1902. Oil on canvas, 33 1/4 x 39 5/8 in. Promised gift of Elie and Sarah Hirschfield, Scenes of New York City, IL2021.51.12
Printed with permission from the New York Historical Society

The moral right of the author has been asserted.

ISBN 978-1-915553-27-0

**Nederlands letterenfonds
dutch foundation
for literature**

Shoestring Press gratefully acknowledges the support of the Dutch Foundation for Literature.

ACKNOWLEDGEMENTS

Translations in this collection, or earlier versions of these translations, have appeared in the following publications:
Acumen, *Dutch*, *De Hofjeskrant*, *The Manhattan Review*, *Poetry Review*, *PN Review*, *Tears in the Fence*.

I am grateful to Anthony Runia for his thorough copyediting and to Tom Clifford for his input.

I would like to thank the Dutch Foundation for Literature for providing a translation grant.

Thanks are also due to Toon Tellegen's publisher, Uitgeverij Querido, for permission to print these translations. The Dutch source texts are from Toon Tellegen's collection *Tot de winter er op volgt*, Em. Querido's Uitgeverij, Amsterdam 2021, and from his collection *Langs een helling*, Em. Querido's Uitgeverij, Amsterdam 2023.

CONTENTS

Introduction — 1

TILL WINTER FOLLOWS

Life Has Warped	9
The Face of Old Age	10
Nothing Comes to an End	11
Small Demons	12
On the Other Shore	13
Self-Portrait with No Explanation	14
Oh, and so on and so Forth…	15
One Morning in March	16
My Dog and I	17
Playing Field	18
Reality with Silence, Sun and Happiness	19
List of Brilliant Things	20
Somewhere Along the Way	21
Righteousness on My Side	22
Sunset in the Attic	23
Twittering Homebirds Made of Paper	24
Losing Face	25
The One Real Must	26
My Mind Stumbles, Looks Around	27
The Promise	28
I Will Miss My Dog Terribly	29
I Don't Trust Myself	30
'Old Man with Lightning and Mimosa'	31
Evening Falls on Its Knees	32
The past Takes to Its Heels	33
Going up in Smoke	34
A Bedtime Story	35
The Opposite of Me and You	36

Write on Walls	37
Where Is Everybody?	38
The Muses	40
At the Cutting Edge	41
The Prodigal Beach Comes Home	42
To A Baseball Game with Walt Whitman	43
Me and My Thoughts	44
Holes in the Mind	45
All Numbers Smaller than Two	46
The Decisions	47
Flying past at Sunrise	48
What Shall We Do	49
Thinking About Everything	50
The Scent of Pale-Pink Liquorice	51
Artist with Sleeping Dog	52
I Stayed on the Main Road	53
Love… Can You Spell That?	54
Did You Have Time for Me?	55
My Last Words	56
She Was Right Behind Me	57
To Be Outside, Singing	58

A SLIPPERY SLOPE

A Slippery Slope	61
In Summer	62
When I Was Young	63
All the Things I Wanted	64
Life	65
Long Ago	66
Between War and Being Born	67
Early Poem	68
On the Way	69
Evening	70
Thoughts	71

I Went on a Journey	72
July	73
Time	74
Questions	75
Quarrels Live	76
Threat	77
In the Middle of Our Life	78
Gradually	79
Saving the World	80
Under a Streetlamp	81
At a distance	82
Held up to the Light	83
Spring	84
Late One Evening	85
For the Last Time	86
Just Leave Us Be…	87
People Waiting	88
The Value of Life	89
A Straw	91
Autumn	92
I Grew Old	93
Old Age Is Everything	94
Old Man in Vegetable Patch	95
Old Man with No Way Out	96
Old Man and Angel	97
Hidden in the Bushes	98
Life Is Beautiful	99
Supplication	100
At the End of Our Life	101
In A Small Church	102
My One-but-Last Poem	103
A Black Hole	104

INTRODUCTION

Toon Tellegen is by now an internationally-acclaimed writer who, now in his eighties, is as prolific as ever, with a string of new books to his name. His poetry and children's stories, also enjoyed by adults, have been translated into many languages. His poetry has won international awards, his absurdist humour has gained him a wide following in Eastern Europe and Russia, his children's stories have won him prizes in Germany and the UK, his fiction is a hit in Japan.

He continues to give readings of his work, often accompanied by Het Wisselend Toonkwintet, a group of musicians with whom he has performed since 2006.

Tellegen appeals to a wide audience and is one of Holland's most frequently quoted writers. The American poet John Brehm once commented, in a review of Tellegen's poetry: 'It's difficult to imagine a poet whose work is more likely to appeal to admirers of both mainstream and experimental contemporary poetry.'

Born in 1941 in Den Briel, a town in the south-west of the Netherlands, Tellegen grew up in a family of four. His father was the local GP, and Tellegen was to follow in his father's footsteps, studying medicine at the Universities of Utrecht and Rotterdam. He worked for some years as a doctor in Kenya, in Maasai country, before returning to the Netherlands, where he was a GP until his retirement. All the while he found time to write fiction and poetry, and by now has thirty poetry collections to his name.

Tot de winter er op volgt ('Till Winter Follows') and *Langs een helling* ('A Slippery Slope'), published in 2021 and 2023 respectively, are Tellegen's latest collections, in which he explores the challenges of old age with a characteristic mix of light-heartedness and urgency. As the two collections complement each other thematically, it seemed fitting to combine them in one long English collection, divided into two chapters.

In *Till Winter Follows* Tellegen scrutinises 'the face of old age', pondering what lies behind its gnarled features: an unexpected impatience, unanticipated plans, desires and curiosity. Old age is presented from all angles, and death becomes the pivotal force around which the poems move and falter, a haunting presence to be defied, feared, or almost – but never quite – accepted. There are moments of poignant longing, as in 'Evening Falls on Its Knees', which ends with the line 'night, give me a little more time'; there are moments of resistance, and times when the speaker looks back on his life and takes stock, sometimes in the form of lists – and Tellegen's lists are always dynamic, with their components enhancing or bouncing off each other.

In a characteristically minimalist setting, blending elements of fairy tale and everyday life, dream and reality contend with each other, repeatedly clashing and switching places. In the beautiful short poem 'On the Other Shore,' the comfortable, safe shore of reality is to be avoided, and we are admonished: 'in your mind always be on the other shore'. On the other hand, in the poem 'Reality with Silence, Sun and Happiness', it is the 'great, silent unreality' that is ultimately not enough for the speaker, who turns back inside to 'embrace reality.'

In his inimitable style, Tellegen navigates between the earthly and the abstract, between the mundane and the god 'in whom I don't believe', between the concrete and the philosophers he admires and distrusts ('Oh, Schopenhauer, it is more than the will'). Many of the poems are open-ended, steering clear of any lasting solace or serenity. Yet Tellegen's work is never nihilistic, and there is often something indefatigable in his protagonists. The confronting angel central to an earlier collection, *A Man and an Angel*, reappears here in several poems as a force to be wrestled with – and it is a never-ending, yet intimate struggle. The poem 'Righteousness on My Side' concludes with the line: 'and the angel realised I was unbeatable.'

In *A Slippery Slope*, Tellegen again focuses on the challenges of old age, while also looking back on his youth and on the women who played a role in his life. In addition, a number of the poems reflect on his art and on what his writing has meant to him. In the powerful poem 'Long Ago', the speaker suddenly realises that the words tumbling from the sky would become his life, and at that very moment he finds that 'my war became my peace.'

As in *Till Winter Follows*, it is the unpredictable road that is favoured ('I wanted to lose my way'), the impassable path, the prodigal son, the small rather than the large: 'A little is enough for me… I would make that little count for something/I would love somebody with it/and work miracles' ('Life').

Again the tireless angel appears, first in the poem 'Old Man and Angel': 'and they went on fighting, seriously and scrupulously/never did a man and an angel love each other so deeply'; and later in the poem 'At the End of Our Life': 'at the end of our life we sit down with angels,/drink red wine/and forget reality.'

The process of translation was relatively straightforward, as Tellegen's poems seem readily to lend themselves to translation. Working with Tellegen is always a joy, everything is open to discussion and he gives a translator room to manoeuvre. I followed the Dutch closely wherever possible, but when exploring options, I would sometimes choose the word that felt closest to the spirit rather than the letter of the work – of course always in consultation with Tellegen. In the poem 'Long Ago', for instance, which focuses on the first stirrings of his writing, unusual words come falling from the sky and the speaker begins to play with them. In the translation I decided to use words that had little to do with the meaning of the Dutch, but had an equally playful, unusual feel to them (e.g. 'flotsam, fisticuffs').

When I had almost finished translating *Tot de winter er op volgt* ('Till Winter Follows'), Tellegen began to send me new poems, poems that would become part of his next collection, *Langs een helling* ('A Slippery Slope'). I immediately began to translate them, and whenever Tellegen sent me new versions, I'd adjust my translations accordingly. It was interesting to witness how Tellegen is constantly reworking his poems, with each new version becoming tighter and more powerful.

Both collections were well-received by the press. Lisa Rooijackers, in *De Poëziekrant,* writes: 'Winter is at the door, and Tellegen disarmingly addresses his fear of death. The witty passages are offset against more serious lines; Tellegen strikes a beautiful balance, always knowing when to be serious. This collection impresses without overwhelming or intimidating the reader. Tellegen is courageous in his candour, profound in his clarity, comforting in his playful metaphors.'

Kamiel Choi, in *Meander,* compares Tellegen to Szymborska. He argues that Tellegen is unwilling to relinquish his down-to-earth, scientific outlook in favour of a purely lyrical mode, and that it is in the tension between these two poetics that his power lies. He feels that Tellegen is at his strongest when he takes a step back from philosophising and simply *shows* his readers what he has experienced.

Dirk de Geest, in mappalibri.be, comments on how Tellegen creates his own unique universe, in which animals, objects and even abstract forces can talk. He suggests that this generalised personification is the key to many of the poems, bringing the poetic 'I' into closer contact with the world, like a kind of alter ego that talks and thinks like a person, and takes action. This often results in narrative poems in which metaphors assume literal forms and generate absurd mini-intrigues. Yet despite the whimsical, fairy-tale settings, Tellegen is never vague or non-committal.

Janita Monna, in *Trouw,* writes: 'In his long and impressive oeuvre, Tellegen has succeeded in tackling the most complex themes – love, hate, resentment, God, life, peace, death – in poems of a tantalising simplicity. In this latest work, his language is as alive as ever. Tentatively, Tellegen considers what will one day become the smouldering remains of life. But even though the poems sometimes read as an exercise in farewell, it is too early to say farewell to reality just yet: 'don't go! you'll miss me!/what do you want with unreality? what do you know about her?'

It seems fitting to end with a quotation from one of his poems, 'Playing Field', in which the speaker imagines standing on the banks of the Lethe and wonders if he would drink:

> behind me the immense playing field of my conscience,
> where good and evil sleep in each other's arms
> and joy and sorrow attack and devour each other
> till they're obliterated
>
> I need to think,
> I need to start thinking at last
>
> I don't drink.

Till Winter Follows

LIFE HAS WARPED

Life was so fresh, so impeccable, so Sunday-best –
on display in shop windows everywhere.
You pressed your nose to the glass,
how priceless it was, how radiant and righteous,
                    forthright, unswerving…
you couldn't take your eyes off it

it warped while you looked and didn't walk on.

THE FACE OF OLD AGE

The face of old age is not what I expected.
I didn't know there was something behind it: impatience,
evasions, intentions…
It grimaces.
Are those grimaces omens of death
                          or signs of curiosity?
Old age loses its sense of taste, its voice and its longing for the other,
but its curiosity grows, assumes grotesque proportions.
Curiosity about what?

NOTHING COMES TO AN END

Capturing beauty, hanging on to it, embracing it

touching it with your fingertips and seeing it shrink from you,
                                          run away, evaporate

thinking of beauty, growing old and hearing it cry:
'Autumn has come! Make no mistake!'

losing your fear of the tyranny of chance,
seeing your best friend die at the bottom of a pit –
you can hear him tearing himself apart!

            capturing beauty again, hanging on to it and so forth.

SMALL DEMONS

Small demons gently nibble at my ear,
tickle my neck,
whisper things they want that I don't want,
conjure up words, sentences that I shouldn't say,
make me remember what I don't want to remember,
mock me behind my back, with the best intentions,
accompany me everywhere

big demons are too old for all that,
they have their own small demons,
who drop by from time to time
                        for a small, devastating visit.

ON THE OTHER SHORE

In your mind, always be on the other shore

in reality you're on this shore,
well-disposed and level-headed, engaging and reasonable,
deprived of everything that makes life bearable
and unbearable

the river is wide, you will drown, but swim across,
swim across.

SELF-PORTRAIT WITH NO EXPLANATION

I look at myself

I like to exaggerate
and to add something perfectly irrelevant here and there,
and then, when I've finished, I'll draw a speech bubble
                              next to my mouth that says:
'Who am I?' –
as if I don't know
and needn't be ashamed that I want to give the impression
(and am even proud of it)
that I will never answer that question…

I let people look at me –
as if anyone really wants to see me…

OH, AND SO ON AND SO FORTH...

Nonchalance, superficiality, reluctance, awkwardness,
lack of knowledge, lack of nerve, aloofness:
brush them aside,
replace them with light-heartedness and nothing else,
it's not too late!

grab a piece of paper
and write at the bottom: and so on and so forth...

leave the rest blank and go on holiday,
you've earned it

you've earned it! why don't you listen!

ONE MORNING IN MARCH

I am an impassioned petty thief,
I am by turns myself and someone else,
I conduct the minutest reign of terror humanly possible,
I am a regent of the imponderable, a wizard of inadequacy,
I am draped in rags and roses,
I am fuelled by self-reproach and self-defence:
everything I do can be called normal, perfectly normal and authentic

but one morning, one early morning in March,
in the small, sun-baked bedroom of the incomprehensible,
between the smouldering remains of my life,
surrounded by those closest to me, who are weeping softly –
how tidily and unembellished I will lie there then…

MY DOG AND I

My dog and I –
if he could sneer, he'd sneer at all my thoughts:
Spinoza – I don't understand him at all,
he does,
Francis of Assisi – he follows his example,
I don't,
Dante – leaves him cold,
not me

if he could read, he'd read the tracts of the great Hermetics,
                who linger along the borders of the hereafter,
he'd tuck in, as if it was Berliner sausage –
I can't stomach the stuff

he's not afraid of death,
I am

my dog and I –
we are friends, I know that,
he doesn't.

PLAYING FIELD

If I stood on the banks of the Lethe,
would I drink?

I know exactly what I want to forget,
but do I really want to forget it,
do I want to stop feeling the pain of it?

behind me the immense playing field of my conscience,
where good and evil sleep in each other's arms
and joy and sorrow attack and devour each other
                                    till they're obliterated

I need to think,
I need to start thinking at last

I don't drink.

REALITY WITH SILENCE, SUN AND HAPPINESS

Reality:
to say goodbye to her you need to put on your coat,
winter has come, there's a storm on the way, black ice

She tries to stop you:
don't go! you'll miss me!
what do you want with unreality? what do you know about her?

you need silence, some sun through the clouds
and happiness, lots of happiness

it's all there: silence, sun, happiness,
you'll find it all in the great, silent unreality –
it's not enough

you go back inside,
you embrace reality –
she's right.

LIST OF BRILLIANT THINGS

I drew up a list of brilliant things
that I planned to do in my life –
I pinned it to the wall,
it was such a long list…

one day my mother came into my room
and read the list,
she stroked my hair and talked about ruined prospects
and something about pride before a fall and scraping the barrel –
I held my hands over my ears

not long after that, the list disappeared,
perhaps she'd removed it, perhaps I had,
I don't know

I've forgotten what was on the list,
except for the last thing:
to become happy

so that was gone too.

SOMEWHERE ALONG THE WAY

I must have lost her somewhere along the way,
there's no other explanation...

I stop in my tracks

or didn't I bring her with me,
did I simply forget her...

I shake my head

perhaps I haven't looked properly,
perhaps I do have her with me,
among all the things I always carry...

but then surely I'd feel it...
or has she done something to my feelings,
switched them off, 'because of insufficient benefits',
so that I have to reset them...

I linger,
what will I do without her...

I turn back, there's no other way.

RIGHTEOUSNESS ON MY SIDE

For a long time I fought with an angel

whenever the angel grew tired he'd consult God
about the best way to beat, wound or maim me

the God of added value, in his sober alcove,
        where Nietzsche waited on him, made tea for him,
            removed crumbs from his beard

the angel kept coming back to me
with new techniques that I wasn't familiar with
and he demolished me, dragged me after him

but I had righteousness on my side,
draped in the colours of the palaces along the Neva
and the scent of lilacs

and righteousness never left my side, encouraged me,
wiped the sweat off my brow

and the angel realised I was unbeatable.

SUNSET IN THE ATTIC

Sunset in the attic
between cobwebs, dust and mouldered wood

when it's dark, you open an old chest with iron fittings
and there he is:
war,
almost intact and undamaged

he gets up, stretches his limbs,
'how soundly I've slept…!'

steps out of the chest, rubs his eyes,
'how tired I was…!'

walks to the attic window, stands on his toes
and looks out,
the moon rises, a streetlamp comes on,
people are hurrying home

war turns round,
'you hadn't forgotten me, had you?'

TWITTERING HOMEBIRDS MADE OF PAPER

and a roaring elephant made of concrete
that climbs a tree for the umpteenth time,
catches a glimpse of the horizon for the umpteenth time,
pirouettes on one foot out of sheer joy,
loses its balance

and falls for the umpteenth time
on a man of glass
who was dreaming of a girl of linen
for the umpteenth time,
a pale-blue girl of frayed linen,
whom he asks out, begs out, to the seaside, to bed

and who was about to say yes, for the first time, all right,
yes!

LOSING FACE

My grandfather once told me a story about a man
who lost his face.
It happened at a banquet, everyone was laughing
and chattering.
That man, no more than a boy really, said something
that made everyone stop talking and look at him.
Then his face slid off his head and fell on the ground.
What remained was a bloody mass
between his ears and his chin,
and yet no one seemed surprised.
He bent down, crawled under the table to find it,
dabbing the blood with his handkerchief.
Everyone started chatting again, no one helped him look.
His face had rolled away; he found it two chairs further down.
Someone had stood on it and damaged it. It was in a bad way.
My grandfather loved that expression: in a bad way.
God is in a bad way, Russia is in a bad way…
From that day onward, the man's face
bore traces of what had happened.
Whenever he was in company, he'd touch it with his hands
to make sure it was still there.
He turned down dinner invitations
and stayed behind in Russia after the Revolution.

THE ONE REAL MUST

When you're old, you've always been old,
when you're young, you'll always be young,
but when you're dead, you're all things,
and something different every day

children run outside, crying:
'Don't give up! We will never give up!'

I stand in the doorway and watch them disappear,
I'm cold and think:
never giving up is the one real must…

it's a day like any other and I go back inside,
I have one second left to live.

MY MIND STUMBLES, LOOKS AROUND

My mind approaches in its black suit that is a little too tight,
stumbles,
looks around,
cries:
'where have my feelings disappeared to this time? why do those wretched feelings of mine keep letting me down?'

everything about my mind creaks and grates
as it walks on, oblivious of the abyss at its feet.

THE PROMISE

My honour has never blossomed,
it's a daisy that tries to bud in vain
in the shadow of the deadly nightshade that is my conscience,
somewhere on the vast prairie of life and death

I hear the hoof-beats of innumerable buffalos,
the cries of Indians hunting them

my conscience,
I promise nothing.

I WILL MISS MY DOG TERRIBLY

My dog talks about 'my human' to other dogs,
I'm familiar with his irony, his mocking laugh

my dog boasts about me: 'my human isn't up to much,
but he creates poems, and *your* humans can't compete with that…'
the other dogs keep silent at such moments

my dog does things the easy way,
I do things the hard way

my dog wishes I could dance and would dance with him
                                        in the dance-hall of his mind –
I've never set foot in there,
I've never even peeked through a window

my dog wants an amuse-bouche before he gets his pet food,
even just a small shin of beef on a bed of bacon

in the films dreamt by my dog, cats and their criminal behaviour
come to a sorry end

my dog has his own Descartes, a grey bouvier
whose tail points straight up in the air to prove he exists,
and who considers humans an inferior species

my dog gets so tired of me and my nonsense…
barks: 'Down now, be quiet…!'
while pointing at the door with his head

I will miss my dog terribly when he's gone.
What he'll do when I'm gone?
Nothing special, I reckon. After all, humans die.

I DON'T TRUST MYSELF

I don't trust myself,
but I can't quite figure out why

can't figure it out... oh please!

I turn round, the window is open,
a bumblebee buzzes, a pigeon coos

I know only too well why I don't trust myself,
can't trust myself
and never should trust myself,
I can explain it, now

I can't explain it.

'OLD MAN WITH LIGHTNING AND MIMOSA'

I move on and see myself,
I stop and look,
take a few steps back and look again,
then I move on again

I don't know what to make of myself

I see others,
I find them beautiful, ugly, dull, interesting, insignificant and
    quite nice,
I have an opinion about everyone

near the exit an academically trained girl
asks me what I think of myself,
if only I knew, I say,
she ticks a box with my answer

when I go back some time later I've disappeared,
I'm in storage, I reckon,
I no longer need to have an opinion about myself

in my place is a clear winter sky
with two skaters and a red air balloon

everyone finds it beautiful.

EVENING FALLS ON ITS KNEES

Dear night,
I wish you wouldn't come,
I didn't ask you to come, did I?
except for that time when the afternoon snarled at me,
didn't want to know me
and went on being afternoon long after it had stopped being,
but after that I didn't ask you any more,
after that I wanted to last and last:
an evening that would not pass,
with hours that grew shorter and yet longer, lighter,
that's the kind of evening I wanted to be…

who can tell me if morning will return after you?
and what kind of morning, if it does come?

I am tired, night,
you're gently unbuttoning me, I can feel it,
you're already untying my shoelaces…

night, give me a little more time.

THE PAST TAKES TO ITS HEELS

The past takes to its heels,
it's scared of me

I might hurt it,
leave it in the lurch, or forget it

and then go on alone
with only the here and now before me, behind me

I would be weightless,
gone would be those leaden feet, the strained back,
the sudden knot in my stomach

and no more writing, blotting, smudging, fudging.

GOING UP IN SMOKE

I burnt God to cinders,
I was ashamed that I made a fool of him,
rubbed his nose in my dusty soul
and didn't believe in him

he went up in smoke and disappeared

I am cold, I poke about in his remains,
in which I don't believe either.

A BEDTIME STORY

Once upon a time there was a man who fell apart –
it was a non-event

people put him back together again
and examined the result:
he was complete, except for one missing piece, one random piece

no matter how hard people looked for it, they couldn't find it
and told him he should settle for
how he was now

and that man fell apart again
and again,
and each time one piece went missing

until eventually there was nothing left of him
and everyone closed their eyes and slept.

THE OPPOSITE OF ME AND YOU

You and I, we're everything:
vast and narrowly circumscribed,
fitted with all conveniences and inconveniences,
in full bloom and wilted,
impassioned and indifferent,
hopeless and more hopeful than we've ever been

we'd like to be more than all that,
but that's impossible:
more than everything is still everything

we grab each other, knock each other over –
mud splashes, we pant, we're shattered,
but we are still everything

we get up, dust our clothes off, turn our backs on each other
and realise once again:
the opposite of me and you is nothing.

WRITE ON WALLS

Write on walls:
'Oh Schopenhauer, it is more than the will…'

it's pain and mood-swings
that make life unliveable

arriving in their galleons
with one-legged captains and Jolly Rogers

it's poisonous daisies and frivolous snakes
                            in the lush grass of bliss

write your name on walls and let yourself weather.

WHERE IS EVERYBODY?

A small statue of Dante,
a clock in the shape of a pyramid,
a wooden egg with the wooden church of the Transfiguration
   in Kizhi on it,
a hippo carved out of soapstone,
mistakes I have made, avoidable and unavoidable,
shame of a chronic nature,
dictionaries,
a reproduction of a painting by Piccolomini,
an empty chest for a Zeiss microscope from 1925,
a dormant ailment that is biding its time,
a book of Francis Bacon reproductions,
a book of Piero della Francesca reproductions,
a book of drawings by Franciszka Themerson,
a book of Albert Marquet reproductions,
a short novel by Natalia Ginzburg,
a book of drawings by Metka Krašovec,
a paper boy wearing a cap,
a wooden cabin without windows and doors,
a grey mouse with four whiskers made of woollen thread,
a polyester cave olm,
a plastic Tokyo Tower,
a boy made of tin, in a green jacket, handing a pinecone to a
   squirrel,
an iron bust of King William I,
a small round mirror with on the back a hedgehog looking in a
   mirror,
two shells from the beach at the foot of the Ladder on Saba,
a Times World Atlas,
a school atlas of the Netherlands Antilles, Aruba and the
   Caribbean Sea,
an electric heater,
a wooden lamp with a shade lined with yellow ribbon,

an eye floater in my left eye,
two yellowing children's drawings, on one of which is written
    FORE TOON,
impatience, unease, discomfort and restlessness,
guilt, lots of guilt, irredeemable guilt,
a notepad,
a bookmark from Perdu bookshop,
a tin box in the shape of a London double-decker,
a box of IKEA pencils,
Italo Calvino's list of conditions literature must meet,
my own list of conditions literature must not meet,
a red pencil, an ordinary pencil, a ballpoint pen, a ruler, an
    eraser,
a view of a garden at 11.30 in the morning on 14 January 2020,
a piece of stone from the Berlin wall with remnants of graffiti,
a boat-shaped slice of agate bought in Batavia in 1933,
a memory of an afternoon in the spring of 1952,
a memory of a milk churn filled with lemonade and wasps,
a memory of the Strassburger Circus on Kruiskade in Rotterdam,
a marzipan whale from 1978, wrapped in cellophane,
a kind of pen-wiper with the word GRANDPA on it,
a good intention, or in fact a string of good intentions,
    workable and unworkable,
the thought of the song 'If You Leave Me Now',
an imaginary hand strangling me,
a sheet of paper with at the top the words: 'Where Is Everybody?'

THE MUSES

The first one stares at me with her big black eyes,
the second looks like a mouse and in fact squeaks,
the third jeers at me,
the fourth never ran into me,
the fifth puts up an umbrella, she thinks it's raining
                              and blames me for it,
the sixth is my mother,
the seventh stands aside, I make her laugh,
                              but she's not sure she loves me…
the eighth is everywhere and waits for me in vain

I love the ninth, who might read this.

AT THE CUTTING EDGE

I asked myself:
'Why aren't you a better person?'

a question that cut through me like a knife,
dividing me into two halves

it took a long time before I answered,
more than fifty years

around me people died of hunger, violence and self-sabotage

nobody asked me questions any more,
not even I myself

my two halves had grown distant from each other,
but the wounds were still fresh and painful

and one morning, at the beginning of winter, I answered:
'I don't know.'

THE PRODIGAL BEACH COMES HOME

The prodigal beach comes home,
kneels before the sea

the sea has grown old, deaf and blind,
he kisses the beach with his wrinkled lips,
'my beach…' he mumbles, 'oh my beach…',
his breakers weep

behind his back a whale disappears into a box,
the wind lies down on a bed of seagulls,
the water turns black out of gloom and disgust

if only I'd stayed home…
oh mother, star of my past, forgive me…

TO A BASEBALL GAME WITH WALT WHITMAN

I went to a baseball game with Walt Whitman,
he taught me what to see and what not
and when to get up
and shout that the umpire was blind
                            and the second baseman as well,
he explained to me what a double play was
and what I should sing in the seventh inning
and that winning was more important than losing

we were sitting in the bleachers,
he caught a home run for me
and kept slapping me on the shoulder

and when we went home
he said:
now I will show you how to write…

Walt Whitman, why didn't I go with you then?

ME AND MY THOUGHTS

My thoughts want to be free,
I'm in their way

they collect spectres, final warnings and aversion,
they scratch me, bite me, cover me in shortcomings
                                                  and shame,
I deny them freedom

they call my mother for help,
she gets behind me, 'straighten your back', she says, pulling at
    my shoulders,
she strokes my hair

my thoughts let her go again,
they don't know what to do with her

dog-tired, dismal, dejected,
me and my thoughts.

HOLES IN THE MIND

Holes are appearing in the mind

people look through them,
see things they've never seen before:
red shrikes, white sunflowers,
                              tiny, elegant wars,
they want to touch, grab hold,
but their fingers are shrivelled and worm-eaten

they grow frantic and crawl into the holes,
get stuck half-way through,
like Winnie-the-Pooh

they wrench and twist, but no one comes to help them
and they live on, thrashing about, gasping for air –
with death lying in wait:
a fence with a door ajar.

ALL NUMBERS SMALLER THAN TWO

In me are all numbers smaller than two:
they pursue each other, hound each other, almost overtake each
    other

outside in the twilight the others whirl about,
the two, the three, the ten –
'we're making something of our lives,' they cry, 'you should do
    the same…!'

I hear my one and my zero pant,
I feel the monotonous weariness of their existence –
they are my inner being, my essence, my self

one day they will seize each other,
say something to each other that I can't decipher
and multiply together

the answer will be of an unimaginable simplicity.

THE DECISIONS

When I look back I see –
with regret, disappointment, surprise and even a certain relief –
the decisions I did not make

I should have made them,
it's good that I didn't,
but I should have made them

they call out to me, beckon, smile as congenially as possible,
    surely you haven't forgotten us?
    no, I haven't forgotten you,
    but you could still make us, couldn't you?
    no, I can't, it's too late for that
    too late, too late… nothing is too late!

then I look ahead again with fresh courage and uncertainty.

FLYING PAST AT SUNRISE

I thought this was possible:
flying without wings, without thinking,
and without this and that and without him and her…

the sun rises and I have wings,
I can go anywhere I like,
beneath me lies the world, my city, my childhood home,
and all those people who see me flying past
and who wave at me
and would like to join me…

but I don't fly, I think
and my wings are in my way.

WHAT SHALL WE DO

What shall we do –
shall we wait and see, sit back and grow old?
simply grow old?

we sit down, shedding tears freely,
and grow old, terribly old, worryingly old

'what are you doing there?' people cry,
'we're busy growing old,' we reply,
'is that all?'
'no'

they sit down with us, they want the same,
and they grow old with us, quietly, modestly old,
poignantly old,
the old of eternal youth and imagination.

THINKING ABOUT EVERYTHING

At night, under my blanket, I think about everything
that will never be all right again

pitch-black thoughts – mosquitoes they are, bats, hooligans

until suddenly, out of nowhere, I think the improbable
                              or rather, the impossible:
that everything will be all right in the end

and then, immediately, without losing a single second,
I fall asleep.

THE SCENT OF PALE-PINK LIQUORICE

The scent of pale-pink liquorice in spring
and nobody to dream of,
nobody to rouse you

I hear a rustling sound – but it isn't a letter, a dress,
something touches me – but it isn't a hand, a mouth

that scent, it belongs to a wilted arum lily,
and as for spring:
it's raining, it's autumn and it will be autumn
                                      till winter follows.

ARTIST WITH SLEEPING DOG

The artist breaks his paint brushes, shakes his head
and says:
'I am no artist, what on earth makes people think I am…'
he wakes up his dog
and gives him a thrashing

the dog sinks its teeth into him, killing him
and goes back to sleep

the painting he'd started that day
could have been beautiful –
the most beautiful thing he'd ever made:
self-portrait with dog

silence has returned to the studio
as the dust settles

that silence is what he'd wanted to paint.

I STAYED ON THE MAIN ROAD

My brother,
he took sideroads, went looking for danger, got lost,
had adventures,
retraced his steps, but never for long,
looked back, looked sideways, looked up,
was desperately happy,
broke arms, legs,
walked in rain, snow, fog, darkness,
met the most peculiar people

I stayed on the main road,
a willing prey to those who hunt for people
who stay on main roads and miss their brother

at night I hear him cry.

LOVE... CAN YOU SPELL THAT?

I put down my pen and asked God:
'That word You keep talking about – love – which Your apostle
    says is
more important than faith and hope: can You spell that?'
And He looked up.
It was the most impertinent question He'd ever been asked.
He swallowed hard and said:
'No, I can't.'
And for a very brief moment, the world bathed in the sublime
    light of the great godlessness, while I shrugged my
    shoulders awkwardly
and picked up my pen again.

DID YOU HAVE TIME FOR ME?

I was growing old –
some last embers of happiness were still glowing in me

I saw everyone I had loved –
some endlessly and deeply,
others a little and only fleetingly –
and I turned round to leave

but a boy stepped forward,
tugged at my shoulder and asked:
'Did you have time for me?'

'No,' I said –
it was getting dark, but I recognised myself.

MY LAST WORDS

There's one thing I want to say before I die,
I know exactly what it is

but I already know that – when I die –
I won't be able to remember the words

'what I wanted to say is…'
will be my last words.

SHE WAS RIGHT BEHIND ME

I fought with an angel
and the angel struck me down,
put his foot on me and asked:
'Who are you taking with you to hell?'

I was slowly bleeding to death,
                         and lost the light in my eyes,
but I gritted my teeth as never before
and whispered:
'Nobody'

and the angel lifted me up, kissed me
and asked:
'And who to heaven?'

and I pointed at her, she was right behind me.

TO BE OUTSIDE, SINGING

I died outside,
wearing a white coat

it was dark, on the road to Lolgorien,
past Mukulelta,
where a drunken chief no longer knew where he lived

'Do I live here?' he cried,
standing on the roof of a Land Rover –
'No,' someone shouted back from a distance

the road was littered with hubris and happy accidents,
the Southern Cross hung straight ahead of me

I died there,
I wanted to be outside, singing
the way I sang on the quayside of Brielle,
accompanied by a crunching and creaking dredger,
and my mother at the window

but I didn't sing, I was dying,
my coat was covered in blood,
on the road to Lolgorien.

A Slippery Slope

A SLIPPERY SLOPE

I'm sliding down a slope so gradually
that it's as if I'm standing still,
the way the hand of my watch seems to be standing still
when I stare at it

sometimes I even think I'm sliding back,
back upwards,
back to where I was long ago,
to the dark clouds that still hang there,
to the sun that goes on shining there.

IN SUMMER

I had a different head,
I was still young

my father was at his work, my mother had a visitor,
I had promised I'd be quiet

I saw things differently with that head –
life was bigger, sharper too –
I could still turn my head on and off at will

my brother chopped it off,
we were playing guillotine

he stayed behind, alone:
I shrivelled up in his memory,
just as he shrivelled up in my head

that autumn I went to school for the first time.

WHEN I WAS YOUNG

I was always ill,
festivities came and went and I was ill

sometimes I was better, heard people whisper:
'he's not ill today… unbelievable…!'
but that same evening I'd be ill again,
my mother would kiss my forehead,
                    realise I had a fever

once I heard someone say:
'so and so's father is paying the price…'
they were talking about me! I was that so and so whose father paid!
numbers fluttered around him,
                    piled up at his feet –
I was his son, who crossed him out

my mother bent over me
and stroked my hair, softly calling my name

I was always ill.

ALL THE THINGS I WANTED

I wanted to lose my way

When I looked back, I wanted to see the wrong turn
that I'd taken,
I wanted to see people being left behind,
I wanted to see them shake their heads and turn back,
I wanted all their efforts to have been in vain,
all their warnings to have fallen on deaf ears

I wanted not to be the wisest, not ever,
and certainly not to be happy

I wanted to be displaced, dismantled, dislocated, dis-whatever,
not fulfil a single promise,
not meet a single expectation

I wanted to be disappointed in myself,
second-guess myself, despise myself, curse myself

I wanted to be the prodigal son
who was never heard of again

I was still young, I wanted everything.

LIFE

As a boy, I started reading poems,
they showed me the scope of a full life

I wanted a fifth or a quarter at most
and see the remainder disappear into a cloud
                                    of superfluity

people would shake their heads about me,
'how little you live…' they'd say

'a little is enough for me,' I'd reply

I would make that little count for something,
I would love somebody with it
and work miracles

a small miracle from time to time.

LONG AGO

Long ago, the sky was still high and empty,
the days still long and infinite

words fell down, one afternoon,
tumbling around me:
dullard, dottiness, dogsbody, flotsam,
fisticuffs…

I grabbed hold of them,
let them flounder and flutter in my hands,
tied them together and freed them again,
let them fiddle and fool around

and just as suddenly as they'd arrived
they disappeared again, the sky was empty once more

but I knew then – I remember it clearly:
this will be my life!

and my war became my peace
and the sun, my sun, appeared
                          when I asked it to.

BETWEEN WAR AND BEING BORN

Between war and being born the night ends

slugs raise their heads and attack each other
Achilles and Hector before the gates of Stalingrad

don't call me father, God thinks,
why does everyone call me father?
I don't have children

the slugs curl themselves round each other:
hunger! desire!

the sun climbs up
and I, I emerge

will anyone hear me?

EARLY POEM

Ships steer a crooked course across the sea,
helmsmen hold the tiller at a crooked angle

crooked-minded believers break their consciences
over the crookedness of life

the crooked-full claim their crooked-founded place
at the fringes of a teetering society

and in the twilight of a grey day in winter
the last of the just turns off the light.

ON THE WAY

I wish I were walking along a path that was impassable,
that I needed to turn back, but didn't turn back,
instead kept walking, on and on,
not yet knowing the difference between passable and impassable.

EVENING

Anything can grow tired,
people, objects, ideas…

anything can yawn and stretch,
lie down and think (and sometimes even say out loud):
I can't go on…

only gravity can't do that,
it doesn't grow tired,
it makes everything fall
and keep falling
and falling
and falling

it doesn't think.

THOUGHTS

There are thoughts that I don't want to think –
they patiently wait for my usual thoughts to grow tired

I don't know where they hide,
but they keep popping up one by one

if they had a voice they'd yell: 'we're back!'
slap me on the shoulders with the kind of jolliness
I hate

I wish I were strong and brave

that's one of those thoughts:
'you're not strong and not remotely brave!'

they rub that in.

I WENT ON A JOURNEY

I went on a journey,
I didn't want to run into anyone,
but someone crossed my path

'I don't want to run into you,' I said,
'same goes for me,' came the reply

we looked at each other and walked on,
perhaps we wouldn't meet another soul now

but no such luck –
'yet another person,' we said
and the person we ran into sneered:
'you've got that right'

in the end we headed home,
determined never to travel again
and we hid in a basement, huddled up close to each other,
not knowing what was in store for us

'we are two people who ran into each other
against their will,' we whispered

we loved each other

JULY

I am looking for someone to blame,
someone who's done something unforgivable

perhaps I need to start with myself –
I've done plenty such things

one fist slammed on the table is enough
to restore proportion

the red of the poppies in the fields,
                             climbing the slopes,
the blue of the sky, the trembling of the air:
all this tugs at my thoughts

July is too old for me, too beautiful, too ripe,
it expects too much of me

I look for my keys,
I want to go inside

I will stay outside.

TIME

I think time, the passing of time,
is the most mysterious phenomenon that I know.
If God created time and its passing,
I think he's a genius.
If he created the word I think he's uninteresting,
I can do that myself.
If he created life I think he's slovenly
and not fit to be God.
If he created death I think he's sensible,
but no more than that.
If he created himself I think he's stupid,
bordering on imbecilic.
Time, the way it always continues,
      while nothing and no one can disrupt it:
if he created that, I am prepared, once in a while,
at moments *he* doesn't see coming,
just briefly, for no more than a fraction of a second,
to believe in him.

QUESTIONS

Could I ever be completely at the end of my tether,
or utterly dumbfounded?

someone asks me:
'how dare you shrug off all consolation?'

and another says:
'that light-heartedness of yours, just you watch out,
you might lose your footing and blow away...'

and foolhardy, impudent, fashionable and guileful,
could I be any of those, ever?

I must go, there's a quarrel brewing.

QUARRELS LIVE

In the beginning there were quarrels and the quarrels made man
and man quarrelled.
By quarrelling you may help someone into the next life,
who reports from there:
'We have quarrels here too!'
A quarrel's big brother is war, its father rancour,
its mother jealousy.
The first thing you learn: I quarrel, therefore I exist.
When you turn twelve you're given a quarrel for your birthday,
when you turn fifty, regret.
Before going to sleep you pray:
'Deliver us from our quarrels and make us young and amiable
 again.'
Quarrels are fond of tears and Fauré's requiem.

I ran into a quarrel, had never met her before.
'Shall I walk with you some of the way?' she asked.
'Fine,' I said.
It was a beautiful day with thunder, hailstorms
                          and unbelievably sunny spells.

THREAT

Something is about to go wrong,
every day something is about to go terribly wrong

the way the sword of Damocles,
dangling from an unimaginably thin thread above my head,
threatens to fall, every single day,
and doesn't fall

as if something is wrong so that nothing can go wrong.

IN THE MIDDLE OF OUR LIFE

In the middle of our life
bits of damage come to light –
how did they get there?
carelessness? rashness?

we put off repairing them

the damage grows,
modest interventions no longer help

we should replace ourselves,
become someone else, someone we don't know –
who is that? we should think when we run into him,
no idea!

in the middle of our life something manifests itself,
something unbearable.

GRADUALLY

I saw people who, gradually and without any appreciable effort,
became sad

they were so sad, so disappointed too...
like children after their birthday

they came to a halt and looked at me:
was I not mistaken?
were they not happy,
was their life not meaningful, didn't it give them intense joy,
the way looking back on a birthday can be intensely joyful?

they made me doubt what I saw:
perhaps I was confusing sadness and joy,
perhaps no one had taught me the difference between the two,
perhaps I'd never find out

I saw them shrug their shoulders and walk on,
I should mind my own business.

SAVING THE WORLD

I don't think beauty will save the world.
Wisdom won't either, nor freedom, equality, truth,
honesty, determination, altruism,
friendship, courage or loyalty.
I think love will fall short too in the end.
If anything can save the world, it's dullness,
      claggy, treacly, doggedly advancing dullness
with no scent or colour and no beginning or end.
This opinion of mine, in times of war, rising sea levels
and the ever-louder voice of the people,
I call a revelation.
I'm keeping it to myself.
It's absurd, and therefore, above all else, true.

UNDER A STREETLAMP

I saw her standing under a streetlamp
on a street corner,
she was small and carried something under her arm

I looked and saw what it was: her soul,
so *that* was her soul…
I didn't know…

but I was mistaken,
that lamp, that was her,
and that soul was the light around her –
suddenly I saw it clearly

there was nobody in the street,
the lamp she was went out and it grew dark around her,
I couldn't see her any more.

AT A DISTANCE

I saw two girls,
they came to a halt at some distance from me,
casting a sidelong look at me from time to time

they were talking about me,
trying to make me fit their reality,
see me the way I might have been

I wanted to walk on, forget them,
they told me I wasn't capable of that,
and holding up a mirror for each other
they put on some makeup

it was then that I'd never felt happier and unhappier
at the same time –
feelings in balance with each other –
and those two girls became two women,
on high heels,
became day and night, heaven and hell

I run into them everywhere,
they turn to look at me everywhere, casting sidelong glances,
they know my borders
and the swamp on the other side.

HELD UP TO THE LIGHT

Two women
and the one dances in a pink evening dress
and the other gazes out of a window or is asleep or deep in thought
or wondering where I am,
hoping nothing bad has happened to me.

'but something bad *has* happened to me! something very bad!'

and the one smiles, she predicted as much…
and the other can't hear me

two women,
who are lifted up and held up to the light

and the one died young
and the other never existed.

SPRING

Two women are being crucified,
there's a gaping void between them

it's spring and I look at them
without suspecting a higher evil

onlookers ask me: 'what are you doing here?'
'I'm passing the time'
'so are we!'

the two women groan softly
and evening comes

tonight they will be in my dreams,
they will call out to me, but they won't find me –
I don't occur in my dreams

they will be inconsolable,
but no one will believe them.

LATE ONE EVENING

Two women kiss each other, caress each other,
don't know what more they can do,
'we are strangers,' they whisper, 'strangers to each other'

they let go,
oh my god, they think, why is it so difficult
not to be a stranger to those who love us?

they rest their heads in each other's laps,
kiss each other with the passion of the powerless.

FOR THE LAST TIME

At the beginning of winter
two women say goodbye to each other,
embracing each other for the last time

but a moment later they return
and embrace each other again,
'for the very last time,' they say

as night falls it gets colder
and again they return,
'what comes after very last?' they ask

'and after very, very last?'

JUST LEAVE US BE...

Two women implore me:
'please stop inventing us!
just allow us not to exist!'

I know they don't exist,
I know it all too well

but there they are again, time and again,
dreamed up, distorted
and so weary, so angry. so grotesque...

PEOPLE WAITING

There are people who have to wait –
they wait behind windows, before doors, in city squares,
at bus stops, on platforms, in letters, in books,
in each other's arms, in dreams and ideas

there is always someone waiting ahead of them

why are you not here yet… they think
and the sun,
their sun, their heavenly stowaway, castaway, their fiery-red,
                                              drowning sun
goes down

and they go on waiting in the dark, in their sleep,
in the thunder that erupts,
night after night.

THE VALUE OF LIFE

The value of life, based on calculations
and the offsetting of plusses and minuses,
is marginally more than zero,
and in the meantime people are drowning
for a variety of reasons

they want to cry for help, but don't know how –
if they call out too softly, no one will hear them,
if they call too loudly, they will be scolded:
'yes, we hear you all right! we're not deaf!'
and if they call out too often,
no one will bother any more

they clasp treasured items in their arms:
small porcelain vases, exotic sculptures, a woollen jumper

it's a fine day,
far away people are lying in each other's arms in the grass,
whispering to each other that it's a fine day
for the first time in ages!

there has to be an error in the calculations,
the value of life must surely be zero,
even if we can pick and choose our death

those who are drowning call out to each other:
'are there any among us who are desperate?'
nobody answers,
'and any baseless optimists?'
'me! me!'
'and what are you optimistic about against all better judgement?'
'that we will be rescued'

the sun disappears,
people in the grass let go of each other and get up,
dust off their clothes,
they'd expected more from this day,
'but never mind,' they say, as they put on their coats
and head home.

A STRAW

Perhaps I am a straw
and right now, far away, someone who doesn't know me
is trudging along wearily

perhaps I was left behind in a giant stubble field,
where an indignant wind rages at me
and clouds of betrayal brush across me

perhaps I am that straw
and someone is trudging along a path towards me.

AUTUMN

There's a dog walking right through me
and another dog
and a jackal
and a pack of hyenas

people flow towards me to misunderstand me
and then thank me warmly for the entertainment
I offer them

melancholy is a specific modulation of feeling –
in my case an impromptu in c minor
                                    and I am an old, untuned violin

'I love you!' people cry –
how absurd…

the sun goes down,
the wind rises –
once you get home it's too late.

I GREW OLD

I grew old and saw children running, chatting,
cycling, shouting, checking their mobiles

I realised that the distance between them and me
had become unbridgeable

and I looked in a mirror and said softly to myself:
'but the same goes for the distance between you and me!'

OLD AGE IS EVERYTHING

Dealers in humility and humiliations
offer their goods for sale,
their customers kiss their feet

it's going to be a stormy day, a lot of people will die,
there's no escaping it…

the sun breaks through, and standing in doorways are the
spokesmen for controlled indifference,
who call out to me: 'we know everything about you!'

enemies on horseback, their lances level,
on scooters, with brand-new Kalashnikovs,
on stilettos, with bright-red lips…

old age is everything,
but I'm not at home.

OLD MAN IN VEGETABLE PATCH

A man stood still
between the lettuce and the leeks in his vegetable patch –
his chickens cackled,
his guinea fowl scratched about

he looked around him –
what's up… he thought, what is happening…?

then he knew:
he hadn't thought about death for a quarter of an hour,
fifteen minutes, fifteen whole minutes…!

he wondered what he should do, should he be happy?
count himself lucky?
or just start thinking about death again,
as if nothing was up?

and he went on weeding his garden,
tying up the beans, pruning the hedge
and with his customary fear and curiosity
he thought unceasingly about death.

OLD MAN WITH NO WAY OUT

Perhaps it's just as well, he sometimes thought,
as if to comfort himself
,,,,,,,,with something he didn't believe in

words so unwarranted…

and time gorged on him,
wolfing him down, smacking its lips,
almost ready to lean back and relax,
time had almost finished him.

OLD MAN AND ANGEL

'Why don't you leave me alone?' a man asked,
'I can't,' an angel said

they had been fighting clumsily and stoically
for as long as the man could remember

'I am almost dead,' he said,
'that's irrelevant,' said the angel

the man shrivelled up an began to stoop

'and once I'm really dead?' he asked.
'we'll see about that when the time comes,' said the angel

and they went on fighting, seriously and scrupulously

never did a man and an angel love each other so deeply.

HIDDEN IN THE BUSHES

Hidden in the bushes – old man that I am –
I see death:
he's naked, steps into the water, it's a warm day

doesn't he have anything to do today?
I can think of someone...

he swims,
beautiful monster,
friend who isn't a friend

I slink off before he spots me –
as if he could lose sight of me even for a second...

LIFE IS BEAUTIFUL

People are dying, in front of me, next to me

and life goes on being beautiful,
so beautiful and seductive,
as if incapable of being anything else

if it had even a modicum of decency
it would be ugly and repulsive
and rebel against itself

it seems to be dancing, in front of me, behind me,
whipped up by the dead
who keep falling
(and laugh up their empty sleeves).

SUPPLICATION

A man on his knees,
praying to someone he doesn't know:
'give me this day my daily bread and an escape hatch'

he gets that bread, more than he can eat –
he's buried under it, he's overpowered by the aroma

and while he's choking on the bread,
which keeps pouring down on him,
he hears a voice whispering in his ear:
'that escape hatch – what do you want that for?'

AT THE END OF OUR LIFE

At the end of our life an angel approaches us,
blocking the way

'step aside,' we say, 'we need to move on, we're nearly there'

he shakes his head –
behind his back the endless emptiness of true reality,
'you have no business there,' he says

'and what about death? is death not there?' we ask,
'death is nowhere,' he shakes his head again
and flaps his wings

we want to unmask him, clip his wings, smother him,
but we've grown so weak…

then he lays his wings aside, wraps his arms round us
and offers us a drink

at the end of our life we sit down with angels,
drink red wine
and forget reality.

IN A SMALL CHURCH

It has to be in a small church,
with a handful of people

outside Walt Whitman trots past on his white horse,
his barbaric yawp reverberating against the houses

inside everyone is given a pair of slippers
as they sit in a circle round a small heater

God is late, he couldn't find the place,
but never mind –
'we waited for you,'
we know we need to be gentle with him,
if we startle him he might break –
there's still room for him at the back

it's winter,
one of us is dead

'that's why we're here'

some grumble: 'oh really? is that why we're here?
couldn't you have told us sooner?'

'no, and now be quiet, be sad!'

and in that small church, beside a drainage canal,
life loses its lustre,
silence falls, even in the world outside,
only the heater goes on burning

this is how we've planned it.

MY ONE-BUT-LAST POEM

My last poem should be long and ungainly,
as if it were my first poem

it should retroactively cast a stark light
on all my poems

I should die before I can rip it up

it should say something
that I'd never wanted to say under any circumstances

I wrote my first poem on 13th March 1957,
I could have left it at that.

A BLACK HOLE

And one day, long ago, I fell into a black hole
that was so tiny I couldn't crawl out of it
back into the daylight,
but got stuck halfway through
in a peculiar kind of twilight

what am I doing here? I've been wondering ever since.